Becoming a Buddhist

*Discover How to Become
a Buddhist with this Essential
Guide to the Beliefs,
Principles, and Practices
of Buddhism*

by Bano Laurent

Table of Contents

Introduction

Thousands of years ago, a Jain master named Upali engaged the Buddha in a debate. At the end of it, the Jain was so impressed he decided to convert to Buddhism. The Buddha told Upali that he was being too emotional and that he should think about it some more. This only impressed Upali even more, so he wanted to convert right then and there. The Buddha refused, however, insisting that Upali had to learn more.

The Buddha's teachings spread far beyond Nepal and have been adopted by many different people. This is why it's a diverse religion with many different sects, beliefs, traditions, and practices. Adding to that variety are the recent westernized versions that have begun to spring up.

What unites them all, however, are the central teachings of the Buddha. What separates them though, exactly how those teachings are to be understood and practiced in daily life.

To get to the heart of what he taught, we have to turn to the Kālāma Sutta ("sutta" means scripture). When the Buddha was passing through the village of Kesaputta (today's town of Kesariya), members of the Kālāma tribe asked him how to separate truth from fiction.

He said: "*Do not believe in what has been repeated by many, nor in tradition, nor in rumor, nor in what is written in scripture, nor in surmise, nor in axioms, nor in specious reasoning, nor on biases toward something that has been pondered over, nor in another's seeming ability, nor upon the thought that 'this monk is our teacher.' Oh Kalamas, when you yourselves know: 'these things are good; these things are not blamable; these things are praised by the wise. When observed and done, these things lead to benefit and cause happiness.' These are the things that you should practice and abide by.*"

So don't believe in anything unless and until you've investigated it fully, never mind how impressive others say it is, and never mind how impressive you think it is. You should even doubt the Buddha's teachings. The Buddha is not a god. He won't save you, grant wishes, help with that promotion, or get you that parking space.

In this book, I'm going to give you an in-depth overview of Buddhism as together we walk through Buddha's teachings, beliefs, and principles.

Chapter 1: Theravada Buddhism versus Mahayana Buddhism

The year after the Buddha died (543 or 542 BC), his disciples set up the First Buddhist Council to codify his teachings. Unfortunately, they focused on the monkhood and not on ordinary people. It took another century to address this problem at the Second Buddhist Council in Vaiśālī (now an archaeological site in Bihar).

By 269 BC, much of modern day India was united by the Emperor Ashoka, who was sickened by the bloodshed he caused. He converted to Buddhism and though he preserved its original teachings, he also contributed to the current schism.

By his time, Buddhism had changed, becoming more like the dominant Hindu religion. Kandahar (now in Afghanistan) was part of the Greco-Buddhist Kushan Empire (Greeks who converted to Buddhism). Because of Hellenic influence, they made statues of the Buddha in direct defiance of his orders. Some even deified the Buddha, equating him with Apollo (the sun god).

So in 250 BC, Ashoka set up the Third Buddhist Council in an attempt to get back to the basics, defrocking those who disagreed with it. He also sent missionaries (which the

Buddha also didn't like) to other countries such as Sri Lanka, China, and the rest of Southeast Asia.

Theravada literally means "Old/Elder School/Doctrine" in Pali (the language of the Buddha) and: (1) limits itself to the old canonical scriptures taught by him, (2) uses Pali, (3) has a number of common rites, albeit with many regional variations, and (4) no longer observes the ban on images of the Buddha.

Theravada is the dominant religion in Sri Lanka, Cambodia, Laos, Thailand, Burma, and Vietnam.

Mahayana literally means "Big Vehicle" and is incredibly diverse. It accepts: (1) scriptures written after the Buddha, (2) regional gods and goddesses, (3) saints, (4) bodhisattvayānas — beings who put off nirvāṇa in order to help others, and (5) uses local languages.

Mahayana is dominant in China, Japan, Korea, Singapore, Taiwan, Tibet, Bhutan, Nepal, Mongolia, as well as parts of eastern and southwestern Russia. Major sects include Chan, Zen, Nichiren, Tibetan, Vajrayana, and so many more.

To Theravadans, Mahayanists are pagans pretending to be Buddhists. To Mahayanists, Theravadans are bible-thumping literalists. Fortunately, they have a long history of getting along, evidenced by the lack of sectarian wars that have plagued other religions.

Chapter 2: Understanding Dukkha and the Five Aggregates

The Buddha achieved enlightenment in Bodhgaya. He then made his way to the city of Sārnāth where he met five holy men who realized that he'd undergone something profound. They asked him to explain what he knew and the result was his first lecture, preserved today as the Dhamma Chakkap Pavattana Sutta (Setting in Motion of the Wheel of Dharma Scripture).

In it, the Buddha explains the Four Noble Truths, which revolve around dukkha. In the Majjhima Nikaya (Collection of Middle Length Discourses), he said that *"I have taught one thing and one thing only, that of dukkha and of the cessation of dukkha."* (1.140)

"Dukkha" can mean "dissatisfaction," "anxiety," or "suffering." It is so central to Buddhist thought that it deserves its own chapter.

In an ideal world, everything works out for us perfectly. We always get what we want when we want it, never get hurt (physically and emotionally), never get sick, never get old, and never die. Unfortunately, this never happens.

To be born is to enter a world of pain, suffering, and disappointment. That's just the way it is. It doesn't matter how rich or poor you are, or even how optimistic you generally tend to be. You will get scrapes and bruises, you will get sick, you will never get everything you want, things and people will disappoint, and you will eventually grow old and die.

To be a Buddhist, therefore, you must first accept these facts. There is no prayer, ritual, talisman, amulet, power, or god that will save you from dukkha.

Dukkha can be understood as the dissatisfaction, anxiety, or suffering caused by:

1) The futile struggle for permanence, predictability, or stability.
2) Constantly changing circumstances.
3) Frustration, hardship, pain, illness, old age, and death.

The only thing that can be said with any certainty about your life is that dukkha happens and then you die.

The Five Aggregates

To explain why dukkha is an inherent part of life, the Buddha explained that we are all made up of five major bundles called Pancha Khandha (Sanskrit: Pancha Skandha).

1) **Rupa** (form/matter): Our bodies are made of matter, which reacts to temperature, is affected by other objects, and is subject to many limitations. We therefore suffer when it's too hot or too cold, don't have enough food or water, etc. Matter also decays, which is why we grow old, get sick, and die.

2) **Vedāna** (sensation): We like pleasant sensations and dislike their opposite. There's a good reason for this, as pain is how our body lets us know when there's damage.

3) **Sañña** (perception): We all have innate intelligence by which we recognize things and are able to tell one thing apart from another.

4) **Saṃskāra** (habits/impulses): Our personal experiences shape our understanding of the world around us. This affects our personality, as well as our likes and dislikes. Over time, we learn to react to things on automatic, even if we no longer remember or understand their causes.

5) **Vijñāna** (consciousness): This is the unchanging self. Although our personalities, our habits, our likes and dislikes change over time and will continue to do so, vijñāna does not. This is the part of us that observes both ourselves and the world around us uncritically.

These allow us to interact with and understand our environment. However, the way they do so is limited and flawed which makes our perception and understanding imperfect. Train tracks do not eventually meet on the horizon, for example, nor is our world flat. But people believe their erroneous perceptions, so they act accordingly.

While there is indeed an independent reality, we can never truly perceive it. Most of what we think is real is nothing more than mental projections of our flawed perceptions and understanding. To make it worse, our personal biases further deteriorate our understanding of that independent reality.

Most of us therefore live, act, and react to a lot of things that aren't real. Because of the Five Aggregates, we project an illusory world around us, jumping and cringing at the shadows of our own making. Getting sick and hurt are bad enough, but self-inflicted pain and ignorance are worse.

Chapter 3:   The Thirst and Craving of Taṇhā

Taṇhā is "thirst," but it can also mean "craving." This is also central to Buddhism, as it's a major cause of dukkha. There are three types.

1) **Kāma Taṇhā**: Kāma is "desire," and here means an intense craving or even addiction for sensual gratification.

2) **Bhava Taṇhā**: Bhava means "mental disposition," and here refers to an intense craving for continuity, such as continued youth or prolonged life, a state of affairs, or even a relationship or situation. It can also mean a craving for wealth, power, or fame.

3) **Vibhava Taṇhā**: Vibhava means "non-becoming" or "extermination." It can refer to an intense desire to be rid of pain or even a longing for death.

It should be noted that the Buddha did not denigrate all forms of desire. Pali distinguishes between different forms of wanting based on their degree.

Wanting to eat and drink, to be comfortable, to rest and sleep, for example, qualifies as kāmā. Kāmā cannot be denied where such things are concerned, because survival depends on them. Even wanting sexual gratification (so long as it doesn't lead to over-indulgence, deception, force or violence), qualifies as kāmā, since our species must continue.

Chanda translates as "intention," "interest," and even a "desire to act." In Pali scriptures, the Buddha uses "chanda" to refer to wholesome desires — such as the desire to serve others, to protect the weak, and to improve one's self.

Taṇhā, however, is the extreme form of desire that can border on obsession at best, or an addiction, at worst. It is this that the Buddha warned us about.

Unfortunately, not everything translates well from one language to another. Because these gradations of desire are not always carried across well into English, some develop the erroneous view that Buddhists should aspire to be ascetic monks incapable of wanting anything.

Chapter 4: The Four Noble Truths

In "The Setting in Motion of the Wheel of Dharma", the Buddha expounded the Chatāri Ariya Sachānip — the Four Noble Truths.

The First Noble Truth states that: *"To be born is dukkha, to grow old is dukkha, to be ill is dukkha, to die is dukkha. To come across what is unpleasant is dukkha, to be separated from what is pleasing is dukkha. Not getting the things you want is dukkha, as is the five aggregates."*

Another way to understand that is to accept that all things are temporary and therefore inherently unsatisfactory.

The Second Noble Truth: *"Dukkha arises because of taṇhā.*

Because of taṇhā, we are reborn. In being reborn, we experience delight and lust. We seek pleasure here and there, we delight in sensual pleasures. We want to live, but we also want to die."

It is not desire per se, that causes suffering. Rather, it is the unrealistic expectation that temporary things can cause lasting satisfaction. If we pin our happiness on things that will pass, it's only inevitable that our happiness must also pass.

The Third Noble Truth: *"To end dukkha, there must be the remainderless fading away and cessation of taṇhā, the giving up and relinquishing of it, freedom from it, non-reliance on it."*

"Remainderless" is a poetic way of translating the original, but it explains why some habits are almost impossible to break. Until we can get to the real causes of our cravings and uproot them completely, we can't easily break away from them.

The Fourth Noble Truth tells us that there's a way out. You can better understand the Four Noble Truths as follows:

1) Existence is filled with dukkha

2) Dukkha arises because of taṇhā and ignorance

3) To end dukkha, one must end taṇhā and ignorance

4) To end taṇhā and ignorance, one must follow the Eightfold Path

The Four Noble Truths form the basis of Buddhism, over which Theravada and Mahayana are in complete agreement. The Eightfold Path forms the practice, which is where disagreement comes about — even within the same branch.

Since these four form the nexus of Buddhism, it's important to look into them further.

The First Noble Truth

When you can truly accept that dukkha is inevitable, you gain three powerful tools. First, you understand that the odds are stacked against you. Second, you realize you'd better do something about it. Third, since it piles up, you'd better start doing something about it right now. The problem is that most would rather avoid suffering, which is perfectly understandable. Unfortunately, this is how problems stick around and accumulate.

The First Noble Truth asks us to confront suffering bravely. What does your suffering feel like? How does it taste, smell, look, sound? As you read these words, are you comfortable or uncomfortable? Are there loud noises which annoy you? Have you been through something unpleasant which still bothers you? Is there something you should be doing instead of reading this?

Say you have a deadline, but it's so stressful you'd rather do something else. How does that make you feel? Uncomfortable? Is it physical, like a painful knot in your gut? Is it mental, like a vice grip around your head? Both? Are you sick? If so, where does it hurt? Is the pain intense, mild, or does it come and go? Dukkha sucks, doesn't it?

No, please don't run away. Stick with it for a moment — Buddhism isn't for wimps. Nor is it about comfort. It's about facing the facts. One of those facts is that everything is transitory, even suffering. Like everything else, discomfort (physical or emotional) has its life cycle. Rather than run away from whatever is causing you distress, stick with it for a while (unless it's an axe-wielding lunatic).

This is called shamatha (insight), an attempt to accept things as they really are. Don't try to rationalize the cause of your discomfort or beat yourself up over it. Simply accept that you're not happy with whatever is happening. Do not blame yourself, someone else, or circumstances; nor should you start fantasizing in order to cope. Just accept that things aren't too good right now.

The First Noble Truth states that whatever crap you're going through is truth. Any attempt to run away from it will only make it worse. It doesn't matter if your dukkha is of the body, the mind, or the heart. The more you face up to it, the better off you'll be.

Rather than become a pessimist, however, it should encourage you to appreciate things more. Enjoy your youth and health because they'll fade. Stop taking your loved ones for granted because they won't be around forever. Appreciate the good moments with greater relish because they won't last. When bad things happen, understand that they will also pass.

The Second and Third Noble Truths

Kāmā can be healthy, chanda can be good, but taṇhā causes us to lose perspective. In the grip of taṇhā, our relationship with something or someone we want is no longer about satisfying desire. It becomes an exhausting chase for fleeting pleasures, or an attempt to avoid unpleasant things.

Say you want a car because public transportation in your area is awful. So you get a good one at a great price, and you're happy. But then a better model drives past, so now you're unhappy. It doesn't matter that you can now get around better and that you got a fantastic deal. Your day is ruined.

So you trade your car in for a better model, even putting yourself into debt. But then an even better model drives past, so there you are back to square one. Except that now, your debt has gone up.

Somewhere along the way, you stopped wanting a car and instead became obsessed with status and one-upmanship. What the heck does that have to do with getting from point A to point B?—absolutely nothing. Even when you got what you wanted, it didn't bring happiness (at least not a lasting one), because your taṇhā overtook your original kāmā. (Now do you understand why Theravadans insist on using the original Pali?)

Desires will never end because they're part of the human condition. The desire to learn Buddhism, to meditate, and to achieve enlightenment are all desires, after all. It's all a matter of perspective.

Taṇhā stems from our innate need for stability and order, which is self-defeating because none exists. Taṇhā also arises because of our innate revulsion toward dukkha, which is also self-defeating because it's part of life.

The Third Noble Truth therefore sounds insultingly simple. If we could end taṇhā, wouldn't we have done so already?

That brings us back to the First Noble Truth — learning to accept things as they really are and not as we want them to be. Unless and until we stop projecting our false image of the world upon the real one, we'll remain victims of our own ignorance and impulses.

Fortunately, there's the Fourth Noble Truth.

Chapter 5: The Eightfold Path

The Buddha did not invent this, but took it from a far older tradition. Buddha is not a name, but a title held by many others before him. The man who founded Buddhism was Siddhartha Gautama. To distinguish him from the others, he's called the Shakyamuni "Sage of the Shakya" (the tribe he came from and which still exists).

According to the Shakyamuni, it was by following the Eightfold Path that he achieved the self-knowledge which led him to enlightenment. Buddha means "awakened" or "enlightened one," which is the goal of all Buddhists.

The path is meant to be practiced as a single whole, whenever and wherever possible. To better understand it, it's divided into three sections.

a) **Wisdom**
   1) Right View
   2) Right Intention

b) **Ethical Conduct**
   3) Right Speech
   4) Right Action
   5) Right Livelihood

c) Concentration
6) Right Effort
7) Right Mindfulness
8) Right Concentration

The universal symbol of Buddhism is therefore a wheel with eight spokes, called the Dharma Chakra (Wheel of Virtue). The order does not dictate their importance, since all are considered of equal value. Each supports and enforces the others, like the fingers of a hand. The better you can follow each step, the more skillful you're considered to be.

If you say something deliberately hurtful, for example, it's because you're not skilful enough in Right Intention and Right Speech. If what you say is clumsy, you're not skilful enough in Right Speech and Right Effort.

The better skilled you become at the Eightfold Path, the better your control over yourself becomes. And the better skilled you become at controlling yourself, the greater your control over your life becomes. Why? Because your life is a projection of your mind upon the world.

Think of the path as a checklist by which you can measure your progress toward enlightenment.

Wisdom

Wisdom is not book knowledge, but an understanding gained through experience. The First Noble Truth states that there are things beyond your control, so to get ahead, you must look out for the things you can. To do so, you have to take a more critical look at yourself, the world, and how you relate to it.

Right View

In the Kālāma Sutta, we are told to question everything: the Buddha's teachings, what our leaders tell us, even what our experiences have led us to believe. Dogma, culture, traditions, and personal biases bind us to a narrow world view.

We therefore identify strongly with our race, culture, nationality, religion, school, political ideology, etc., believing they define us and the world. They do not. We make ourselves and the world around us, create the rules which define winners and losers, and rejoice or otherwise depending on which side we land on.

Until you question yourself, your assumptions, your beliefs, and your values, you will remain a victim of yourself and others. You must therefore strive to keep your mind calm, rational, and open-minded by avoiding dogma and staying alert to knee-jerk emotional reactions.

The more you practice this, the more you understand how much of your own dukkha is self-imposed, artificial, and fleeting.

Right Intention

With a calm, relaxed, and open mind, you begin to understand that everyone around you is also a victim of dukkha, even those opposed to your beliefs and way of life. Like you, they seek happiness and wish to avoid pain.

So you must therefore think, speak, and act with a kind heart, understanding that even those who aren't kind are the victims of their own dukkha. Those who lash out at you aren't actually being mean to you — they're lashing out at their own mental anguish and you just happen to be in the right spot.

Do not intensify their pain by lashing back. You'll only hurt yourself further by losing your equanimity.

Ethical Conduct

From thought and intention, we move to action. Good thoughts are nice, but they don't do squat for the world unless you act on them.

Right Speech

Don't lie, gossip, insult, or put others down. It's not just about being diplomatic and being careful with others' feelings. Speech is how we communicate and make a mark upon the world. If the world you project is full of lies, gossip, and insults, then that becomes your reality.

What you think, so you say; and what you hear, so you believe. The more control you exert over your thoughts and intentions, the greater your control over your speech. The more you can control these, the more you can control your beliefs, the world you project, and how you live in it.

Right Action

This is an extension of Right Speech, and includes refraining from theft, violence, murder, and sexual misconduct. The latter is open to interpretation, but if you have to use lies, exploitation, violence or the threat of it to get sex, and if you do so with no compassion or concern for the person involved, then it's a no-no. Right action also includes generosity, service, and charity.

Right Livelihood

Scripture frowns on fraud, businesses involved in violence, weapons, killing, slavery, illicit sex, intoxicants, and poisons.

Concentration

Right View tells you how to think. Right Intention guides the process of Right Speech, Right Action, and Right Livelihood. The following, is what ties it all together.

Right Effort

This is the attempt to make virtue your dominant character while being easy on yourself. Your goal is to think, speak, and do good with little effort. With enough practice, the struggle between wanting to do good and actually doing it become less. When you are skillful enough, that gap vanishes completely.

When learning any skill, it's only natural that you'll fall flat several times. But just as others deserve your patience and kindness, so you should be patient and kind with yourself.

Right Mindfulness

This requires you to constantly be aware of everything you think, say, and do. It also requires you to pay attention to what you feel as these things happen. There are a number of meditation exercises which help you achieve this mindfulness, the goal being to prevent you from thinking and acting on automatic mode.

Right Concentration

There are many techniques available, but the two that Theravada focuses on for lay people are:

Vipassana: This requires you to simply focus on your breathing. Whenever thoughts, feelings, images, sensations, and memories arise, bring your mind back to your breathing.

Mehta Bhavana: This teaches you to focus on someone you love and enjoy the feeling that the thought of them brings. You then take that love and try to feel it for someone you neither like nor dislike. The final phase is taking that love and trying to feel it for someone you dislike.

Chapter 6: The Impermanence of Nibbāna

"Nirvāṇa" is Sanskrit, while "nibbāna" is Pali, but they mean the same thing: "blown out." This is not heaven, but a condition where the fire of your passions no longer burn. In this state, you cease to be a slave of your emotions, ignorance, and preconceived notions.

This doesn't mean you're incapable of emotions, only that you're in control of them. When beauty and ugliness, likes and dislikes, fear and attraction no longer rattle you, you become at peace. It's a lot more complicated than that, but it's important to understand that nibbāna is to be achieved here and now, not in some afterlife when you're dead.

The Buddha taught that there are Three Marks of Existence, which explains how the Four Noble Truths and the Eightfold Path come together to propel us toward nibbāna.

1) **Anicca** means "impermanence," so you must strive to walk a middle way, avoiding extreme actions, views, ideas, and beliefs.

2) **Dukkha** has already been covered.

3) **Anattā** means "no-self." You are not who you believe you are, nor are you your impulses, habits, personality, etc. Who you were as a child, who you are now, or when drunk, upset, unconscious, when you suffer from amnesia, etc., are only a bunch of temporary mental constructs.

Put together, they seem to make a coherent whole, but they're not. There are gaps in your memory, entire decades you no longer recall. Nevertheless, you believe in your continuity and fear its end.

The doctrine of anattā teaches that there is no real "I," only fragments of temporary mental constructs strung together to create the illusion of continuity. A dream, no matter how disjointed and illogical, makes perfect sense and seems so real when you're dreaming it.

Nibbāna is waking up from that dream and letting go of the illusion you have made of yourself and your resulting delusions about the world. Who is it that fears pain and death? You? Where are you? Not your body, but that sense of "I" that you have. Where is it? Point to it. You can't, because it doesn't exist.

Understanding that is awakening — Buddhahood. Dukkha ends because the fire of your false projections dies. With it goes the shadow play that caused you so much suffering.

Chapter 7: Focusing on Puja

Puja means "formal worship" which involves prayers and rituals. In Theravada, puja is about focusing the mind so it remains on the Three Gems: the Buddha, the Dhamma, and the Sangha (community of Buddhists).

Most Buddhist homes have a shrine with a picture or statue of the Shakyamuni on it. This is usually decorated with flowers which represent impermanence, since they'll fade and die. Incense is burned to symbolize the fragrance of the dhamma, and a candle is lit to depict enlightenment.

For those wanting to officially convert, the Three Refuges is the entry ticket. Most pujas start with it. There are many other prayers, but the following is the most common daily rite. Puja is usually done in the morning before breakfast and serves as an introduction to meditation or study of scriptures.

Three Refuges
Homage to him, the exalted one, the worthy one, the supremely enlightened one.
I go to the Buddha as my refuge,
I go to the Dhamma as my refuge,
I go to the Sangha as my refuge.
For the second time, I go to the Buddha as my refuge.
(3X)

For the third time, I go to the Buddha as my refuge. (3X)

Five Precepts

I vow to abstain from destroying living creatures.

I vow to abstain from taking anything not freely given.

I vow to abstain from sexual misconduct.

I vow to abstain from false speech.

I vow to abstain from intoxicants which lead to carelessness.

The Four Immeasurable Thoughts

May all sentient beings have happiness and the causes of happiness;

May all sentient beings be free from suffering and the causes of suffering;

May all sentient beings never be separated from the happiness that knows no suffering;

May all sentient beings live in equanimity, free from attachment and aversion.

Sadhu! Sadhu! Sadhu!

"Sadhu" means "well done," and is recited thrice to signal the end of puja. It's also used to mean "bravo" for a performance, a reminder that all actions are a form of practice for self awareness.

Conclusion

Please note that not all Buddhists perform puja or keep images of the Shakyamuni. Others prefer to keep a picture or carving of the Dharma Chakra instead. Still others refrain from reciting the Three Refuges, since they believe it comes too dangerously close to worshipping the Buddha as a god.

For the latter, a shortcut puja simply goes:
"Buddham pujemi, Dhammam pujemi, Sangham pujemi"
(I honor the Buddha, I honor the Dhamma, I honor the Sangha)

Even this, however, is too much for others, who refuse to perform any puja save for daily meditation and the study of Buddhist scriptures. For these people, Buddhism is not a religion, but a philosophy.

Since a number of diverse cultures embrace Buddhism, its practices are equally diverse. However you choose to approach Buddhism is up to you, but whatever you do, you really must learn more than this book can possibly provide. The Buddha himself said so.

If you'd like to meet up with other Buddhists for more information, a good place to start is with the World Buddhist

Directory   (http://www.buddhanet.info/wbd/).   Besides
helping you get in touch with sanghas in your area, they also
have free resources to help you on your way.

Whether or not you choose to embrace Buddhism, may you
be free from suffering and its causes, and may you know
lasting happiness.

Finally, I'd like to thank you for purchasing this book! If you
found it helpful, I'd greatly appreciate it if you'd take a
moment to leave a review on Amazon. Thank you!

Printed in Great Britain
by Amazon